FORENSIC FILES

INVESTIGATING FAKES & HOAXES

Heinemann Library
Chicago, Illinois

. . . . . ALEX WOOLF . . . . .

Originated by Ambassador Litho Ltd
Printed and bound in China by South China
Printing Company

08 07 06 05
10 9 8 7 6 5 4 3 2

**Library of Congress Cataloging-in-
Publication Data**
Woolf, Alex, 1964-
  Investigating fakes and hoaxes / Alex Woolf.
    p. cm. -- (Forensic files)
Summary: Offers a brief history of forensic science
and describes instances in which its techniques
have been used to investigate various crimes,
including murder, identity theft, and art forgery.
Includes bibliographical references and index.
  ISBN 1-4034-4829-9 (hc : acid-free) -- ISBN 1-
4034-5469-8 (pb :
acid-free)
  1. Fraud investigation--Juvenile literature. 2.
Forensic
sciences--Juvenile literature. 3. Criminal
investigation--Juvenile
literature. [1. Forensic sciences. 2. Criminal
investigation.] I.
Title. II. Series.
  HV8079.F7W66 2004
  363.25'963--dc22
                                    2003018155

Acknowledgments
The author and publisher are grateful to
the following for permission to reproduce
photographs:
pp. 5, 22 Michel Viard/Peter Arnold Inc/Science
Photo Library; p. 6 Harcourt Education Ltd.; p. 7
ACO Electronics Ltd; p. 8 Mansell/Getty; p. 9
Science and Society; p. 10 British Library; pp. 11,
25 Gareth Boden; p. 12 Hulton Archive; pp. 13,
14 Peter Kurth; p. 16 Rex Features; p. 17 Mehau
Kulyk/Science Photo Library; p. 18 Boijmans
Museum; p. 20 National Gallery of Canada;
p. 21 Matt Meadows/Peter Arnold Inc/Science
Photo Library; p. 23 Pablo Corral/Corbis; p. 24
Zoe Feast/Indigoimage.com; p. 26 Hulton-Deutsch
Collection/Corbis; p. 28 John Frost Newspapers; p.
29 Sophie Scott/Wellcome Photo Library; p. 30
Stern Magazine; p. 31 Bettmann/ Corbis; p. 32
Geoff Tompkinson/Science Photo Library; p. 33
Klaus Guldbrandsen/Science Photo Library; p. 34
PA Photos; p. 35 Foster Freeman; p. 37
Topham/PA; p. 38 SWNS; p. 39 Volker
Steger/Peter Arnold Inc/Science Photo Library;
p. 40 Topham Picturepoint; p. 41 Dr. P. Marazzi/
Science Photo Library; p. 42 Blair Seitz/Science
Photo Library.

Cover photograph of a painting by Lucas Cranach
the Elder (1472–1553) seen under ultraviolet light
reproduced with permission
of Volker Steger/Science Photo Library.

Every effort has been made to contact copyright
holders of any material reproduced in this book.
Any omissions will be rectified in subsequent
printings if notice is given to the publisher.

Disclaimer
All Internet addresses (URLs) given in this
book were valid at the time of going to press.
However, due to the dynamic nature of the
Internet, some addresses may have changed, or
sites may have changed or ceased to exist since
publication. While the author and publisher regret
any inconvenience this may cause readers, no
responsibility for any such changes can be
accepted by either the author or the publisher.

Some words are shown in bold, **like
this.** You can find out what they
mean by looking in the glossary.

Contents

What Is Forensic Science?

Forensic science is any science used in a criminal **investigation.** Its purpose is to provide scientific evidence for use in a court of law. Forensic science draws from a number of different subject areas: chemistry, biology, physics, geology, psychology (the study of the human mind), and social science (the study of people in society).

What do forensic scientists do?

In a typical criminal investigation, crime scene investigators will gather material evidence from a crime scene. Forensic scientists then examine this material and determine what can be used in the investigation and the trial. Evidence can be anything from the body of a murder victim to the tire tracks of a getaway car. Forensic scientists do not spend all their time in laboratories and offices—they are often called to examine crime scenes, or to appear in court as expert witnesses.

Investigating fakes and hoaxes

Investigating crimes involving fakes and **hoaxes** can involve a number of different forensic skills. A forensic document examiner will usually be called upon in these types of crimes. But fakes and hoaxes do not always involve paper and ink. In one case study to follow, a recorded voice is analyzed to confirm it is that of the person it is supposed to be. In another case, involving a fake painting, **X-rays** are made of the canvas to find out what lies underneath the painting. When a hoax involves a murder, forensic scientists may be asked to examine the body of the victim.

Investigator's toolbox

Forensic document examiners have a number of scientific techniques at their disposal when analyzing a **questioned document:**

1. <u>Paper Analysis:</u> paper has a number of physical and chemical properties that can be investigated. For example, paper fibers can be identified by examining it under a microscope. The most powerful microscopes, such as electron microscopes, can tell an examiner what kind of wood was used to make the paper, and even what species of tree it came from!

There are also very sensitive measuring devices for testing the different densities (concentrations of matter) of paper. One of the things measuring density can help determine is whether a **watermark** is genuine or not.

2. Ink Analysis: sometimes forensic document examiners run tests on ink to discover what it is made of and how old it is, or to reveal writing that has been erased or scribbled out. A technique called **thin-layer chromatography** enables scientists to separate the different ingredients of ink and help identify it. The age of ink can be revealed by measuring how far certain ingredients, known as **solvents,** have evaporated. Erased or written-over ink can often be seen by looking at the document in **infrared** light. In infrared light, certain inks appear luminescent (very shiny), while others appear dark. This process is called **infrared luminescence.** Infrared luminescence can also be used to distinguish between different inks that appear the same in normal light.

These documents are being viewed under **ultraviolet** and infrared light. The light should help provide clues about the documents.

Forensic Science in Action Today

The bank manager studies the check, but he can find nothing wrong with it, except for the odd amount. The signature on the check looks like the signature held in the bank's records. Yet, according to the person on duty, the man who cashed the check in to the bank seemed nervous. The bank manager decides to hand the check over to the local police. The police, in turn, pass the check to a **forensic** document examiner.

Looking for clues

The document examiner's office is full of microscopes and **X-ray** machines. Yet when she is handed the check, she first uses her own eyesight. The human eye can be better than any technical device at picking out things that seem odd or out of place. The examiner has the check photographed alongside an accurate measure, like a ruler. This is to keep a record of the check's appearance, in case any of her later tests alter or damage it. Then she asks the bank to provide her with a handwriting sample from the person who holds that bank account.

A different hand

An examination of the size and quality of the paper confirms that the check itself is genuine, and her tests on the ink show that the same pen was used for all the writing on the check. However, under the microscope she can see something odd about some of the words and numbers. Certain parts have clearly been written more slowly with a different

Every person's handwriting has its own individual characteristics.

pen pressure, and with different starting and connecting strokes. She soon realizes that the check was originally made out for nine dollars, and that the extra words and numbers have been carefully added in. The police are alerted, and later that day the man who presented the check is called in for questioning. A **fraud** has been uncovered thanks to the work of a forensic document examiner.

Questioned documents

The work of a document examiner may not seem as exciting as that of a detective on the trail of a murderer, yet documents can be dangerous. They can be used to mislead people, to take money from them, or even to steal their identity.

Most cases of fakes and **hoaxes** involve **questioned documents.** A questioned document is any written, typed, or printed item that a forensic document examiner studies to decide whether it is genuine. It can be anything from a **counterfeit** banknote to a set of falsified (deliberately altered incorrectly) business accounts, or a faked diary claimed to be that of a famous historical figure.

Forensic analysis can be carried out on paper, ink, and handwriting to establish such facts as the age of the document, who produced it, and whether it has been altered. This analysis has often provided the police with crucial evidence in cases involving fakes and hoaxes.

A questioned document is placed on a shelf beneath this video microscope, and the image is then displayed on the monitor for analysis.

Forensic Science: the Early Days

The history of **forensic** science goes back to ancient times. Handwriting, for example, was studied by the ancient Greek philosopher Aristotle. There is also evidence that the ancient Chinese carried out autopsies (examinations of dead bodies to find out the cause of death). A Chinese book, *Hsi Duan Yu* ("The Washing Away of Wrongs"), written in 1248, tells how to distinguish drowning from strangulation. However, it is only in the last 200 years that science has played a major role in the fight against crime.

One of the first people to apply scientific techniques to the exposure of fakes and **hoaxes** was a Frenchman, François Demelle. In 1609 he published the first essay on **questioned document** examination. Around 200 years later, in Germany, the first recorded chemical test for a particular ink dye was carried out. In 1910, Albert S. Osborne, who was perhaps the most respected forensic document examiner in history, published his landmark work, *Questioned Documents*.

Seeing more clearly

In 1622 Camillo Baldi of Italy wrote the first scientific book about the study of handwriting. The in-depth scientific study of documents—including their paper, ink, and handwriting—could not have happened without the development of equipment to assist vision. The first-known microscope was built in the 1590s by Zacharias and Hans Janssen in Holland. Over the next centuries the power and focusing capabilities of microscopes were improved dramatically.

In 1828, William Nichol invented the polarized light microscope. It allowed scientists to analyze transparent materials in far greater detail than was possible before by measuring changes in the quality of

In 1894 Alfred Dreyfus was forced to write an incriminating letter. The letter was used to prove him guilty of handing military secrets to the Germans. He was pardoned in 1906.

light passing through them. In the 1850s came photomicrography, enabling scientists to take photographs of what they saw under their microscopes. The 20th century saw the arrival of **digital imaging technology,** allowing greater magnification of microscopic images.

X-rays and beta rays

Microscopes could magnify things, but could not show scientists what lay under the surface. For that they had to wait until 1896 and Professor Röntgen's discovery of **X-rays.** X-rays operate at a different **wavelength** than normal light waves, and are able to penetrate solid objects. For the first time it was possible to look at the structures within materials such as paper and paint.

Beta radiography was first developed in the 1950s. This method uses streams of electrons, known as beta rays. Beta rays can penetrate solid objects, but they do not penetrate powerfully, and are easily blocked by things like the fibers within paper. This is why beta radiography is often used to examine **watermarks** in paper. The beta rays are passed through the paper onto a sheet of special film that is sensitive to the rays. More rays pass through the watermark because the paper is thinner there, and the shape of the mark is imprinted on the film.

This microscope is from the 1800s.

A Lost Masterpiece?

The English author and engraver Samuel Ireland was an expert in the works of William Shakespeare. On Christmas Eve, 1795, he revealed to the world that he obtained a collection of manuscripts that, he claimed, were actually written by Shakespeare himself. The collection included a fragment of *Hamblette (Hamlet)*, and a complete manuscript of *The Tragedye of Kynge Leare (King Lear)*, handwritten by Shakespeare. There was also a copy of a previously unknown play called *Vortigern*.

FILE OPEN

Suspicion

People were eager to believe that Samuel Ireland's discovery was real. However, a Shakespearean scholar named Edmond Malone was suspicious. He asked if he could examine the collection. On April 1, 1796, Malone published a 424-page book aimed at fellow scholars and Shakespeare fans on the work, declaring it a fake. He pointed out the spellings of certain words did not match the way such words were written in the 1500s.

M. William Shak-fpeare:

HIS
True Chronicle Hiftorie of the life and death of King L E A R and his three Daughters.

With the vnfortunate life of Edgar, fonne and heire to the Earle of Glofter, and his fullen and affumed humor of T O M of Bedlam:

As it was played before the Kings Maieftie at Whitehall vpon S. Stephans night in Chriftmas Hollidayes.

By his Maiefties feruants playing vfually at the Gloabe on the Bancke-fide.

This is a page from a 1608 edition of Shakespeare's *King Lear*. Ireland claimed to have found the original manuscript written by Shakespeare himself.

Paper chase

Malone also conducted a **forensic investigation** into the paper on which *King Lear* had been written. He discovered that the manuscript contained pages with twenty different **watermarks.** Malone reasoned that Shakespeare, who was already rich and famous by the time *King Lear* was written, would have purchased enough paper of one type as was needed for the entire work. On the other hand, a person wishing to forge an Elizabethan play 200 years later would need to obtain scraps of old paper from wherever he or she could get them—for instance from the flyleaves, or blank pages, of old books.

In May 1796 Ireland's son, William Henry Ireland, published a book confessing to the deception. And in 1805, in another book of confessions, Samuel Ireland admitted that he had paid a bookseller to let him cut out blank pages from the older volumes in his shop. The manuscripts had all been written by William Henry, who was only 21 years old at the time.

Watermarks

A watermark is an image set in a sheet of paper. Watermarks can be used to identify the papermaker because each paper manufacturer creates its own unique watermark.

Watermarks are part of the structure of paper, embedded within its fibers during manufacture—so it is virtually impossible to remove or produce a convincing fake. This makes watermarks very useful to forensic scientists in dating and identifying paper. Forgers have attempted to create fake watermarks by scratching the surface of paper through a stencil with a hard eraser, but the disturbance of the fibers on the surface is easily detectable.

Another method of **forgery** involves printing the mark in olive oil, making the paper look translucent, like a real watermark. However, the edges of marks made in this way are much sharper than genuine watermarks.

The **authenticity** of a watermark can be tested by **beta radiography,** which measures small variations in density in a sheet of paper.

Euro banknotes contain a watermark to make them harder to forge. The watermark shows a picture and displays the value of the banknote.

ECB EZB EKT EKF

20 EURO

Anna or Anastasia?

On July 17, 1918, the Russian Revolution claimed its most famous victims: Tsar Nicholas II of Russia, his wife Alexandra, and their five children. They were murdered on the orders of Russia's new leader, Vladimir Lenin, at a house in Ekaterinburg, Siberia. As the hereditary ruler of Russia, the Tsar and his family could have provided the necessary leadership for a movement to oust the Bolsheviks and restore the monarchy.

The woman in the canal

In February 1920 a woman, who had attempted to commit suicide, was rescued from a canal in Berlin, Germany, after jumping into the water. The woman could not identify herself, so she was taken to a mental institution where she remained for two years. In 1922 she claimed to recall who she was. She announced that she was in fact the Grand Duchess Anastasia Nicolaievna, the youngest daughter of the murdered Tsar Nicholas. The woman claimed that

For two years after her rescue, Anna Tchaikovsky was known as *Fraulein Unbekannt* [Miss Unknown].

she had escaped the massacre with the help of a Russian soldier in the firing squad, named Tchaikovsky, whom she had then married. He was later killed, and she had suffered a mental breakdown before making her way to Berlin, where she had tried to kill herself.

These claims could easily have been dismissed as the ravings of a mad woman. But there were several reasons why the claims were taken seriously. First, the woman, who now called herself Anna Tchaikovsky, bore a remarkable resemblance to Anastasia. She also appeared to have an intimate knowledge of palace life and etiquette. Furthermore, a number of witnesses who knew the late Tsar's family, including the family nurse, identified her as Anastasia.

Comparing photographs

In 1927, Professor Mark Bischoff of the Institute of Police Science in Lausanne, Switzerland, decided to carry out some tests to see if he could prove her identity. He compared photos of Anna Tchaikovsky with those of the duchess. The photos were adjusted in size and one was placed over the other for comparison. Bischoff paid particular attention to the right ear because ears have unique characteristics that can help with identification. There were some differences between the two ears. This suggested to Bischoff that they were not the same woman.

Ear identification

The examination of ears in identifying individuals was first proposed by a Czech doctor, R. Imhofer, in 1906. In 1964 a United States deputy sheriff, Alfred Iannarelli, published a book called *Ear Identification.* In the book, he created a classification system for the characteristics of the ear.

Iannarelli suggested that an individual's ear does not change throughout life, and that everyone's ears are different. Iannarelli's theory remains controversial; not all experts accept that it has a scientific basis.

The National Training Center for Scientific Support for Crime Investigation in Great Britain is now compiling a database of several thousand "earprints" for use in identifying criminals. The organization claims that **cartilage** gives each ear its distinctive shape.

A comparison of Anastasia's (top) and Anna's (bottom) ears showed differences between them.

These retouched photographs of Anastasia appeared in U.S. newspapers in 1928.

Supporters and sceptics

Several Russian aristocrats, who were forced to move and live outside of Russia at the time of the revolution, supported Anna's claim. They hoped she might encourage others to aim for a new Tsarist government, to replace the regime (governing body) at that time. However, there were many others who remained doubtful, including surviving relatives of the royal family such as Tsar Nicholas's mother and his sister, who may have feared that Anna might claim a share of the family fortune.

The doubters pointed to certain weaknesses in Anna's case, like the fact that, although fluent in German, she only knew a few words of Russian. Supporters argued that Anna had forgotten most of her Russian because of the trauma of her ordeal. Supporters pointed to the many physical similarities between the two women. For example, a finger on Anna's left hand bore a scar in the place where a carriage door had been closed on Anastasia's. There was also a scar on Anna's right shoulder where Anastasia had had a mole removed. Like Anastasia, Anna suffered from bone tuberculosis. She also recalled that her aunt, the Grand Duchess Olga, used to call Anastasia *Shvipsik*, a nickname only a small number of family members and servants would have known about.

A new name

By 1928 Anna Tchaikovsky had changed her name to Anna Anderson in an effort to avoid press attention, but the controversy raged on. Over the following decades, she spent time in two mental institutions, and went to court three times in attempts to prove that she was, in fact, Anastasia. In 1968 she married one of her supporters, John Manahan, and moved to Charlottesville, Virginia, where she died in 1984. During her lifetime she convinced many who met her of her story, but was never officially accepted as Anastasia.

So who was she?

If Anna was not Anastasia, then who was she? A theory began to circulate as early as 1927 that Anna Anderson was in fact a Polish-born housewife named Franzisca Schanzkowska. Schanzkowska had been reported missing in Berlin on the same day that Anderson was rescued from the canal.

This theory was first proposed by a private detective, Martin Knopf, who pointed out several similarities between Schanzkowska and Anderson. According to the medical records, in addition to the similarities mentioned above, both women had a history of foot disorders. Knopf also located a witness named Doris Wingender. She was the daughter of Schanzkowska's landlady in Berlin and was willing to identify Anderson as Schanzkowska.

However, Schanzkowska's brother Felix refused to accept that Anderson was his missing sister.

The evidence of DNA

Arguments about the true identity of Anna Anderson continued after her death. In 1985, a new identification technique was developed that promised to solve the mystery once and for all: **DNA typing.** Just before she died in 1984, Anna Anderson had undergone an operation, and the hospital had retained a sample of her tissue. The **DNA** in this tissue could be compared to the DNA of the Romanovs (the Tsar's family) to see if there was a family connection. But what was needed was DNA belonging to the Romanov family.

Finding the Romanovs

DNA typing became a possibility in 1991, when some bodies were unearthed from a shallow grave—possibly where the Tsar and his family were believed to be buried. The first task was to prove that the bodies were in fact the remains of the Romanovs.

Pavel Ivanov, a Russian DNA expert, took the bones to Britain to be examined by the Home Office **Forensic** Science Service, headed by Peter Gill. DNA analysis confirmed that five of the nine skeletons recovered were members of one family. To make a more specific match, the researchers turned to a different test, called **mitochondrial DNA** typing. This test proved beyond doubt that the remains were the bones of the murdered Romanov family.

Missing bodies

Only nine bodies were recovered, though eleven were known to have been shot. The DNA typing showed that the two missing bodies belonged to Crown Prince Alexei and his sister Anastasia. Perhaps they had escaped. This news raised the hopes of Anna

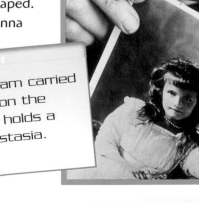

Peter Gill, whose team carried out the DNA tests on the Romanov remains, holds a photograph of Anastasia.

Anderson's many supporters. The supporters approached Peter Gill and asked him to test the sample of Anderson's tissue to see if it matched the Romanovs' DNA.

Mystery solved

In June 1994, Gill flew to the United States in secret to collect the sample. He also obtained DNA samples from members of the Schanzkowska family to see if there was any truth behind the theory that Anderson was actually their missing relative. The following October he announced his verdict: Anna Anderson was not Anastasia. Gill could confirm that she was without a doubt the Polish peasant woman, Franzisca Schanzkowska.

Not everyone has accepted this conclusion. Many of Anna Anderson's supporters have rejected the scientific evidence, and continue to insist that she was the missing Anastasia.

DNA typing

DNA is a type of molecule found in every **cell** of every living thing. Our DNA carries information about ourselves. It is what determines our physical characteristics, and it is what makes us exactly what we are—which is why DNA is useful for establishing identity. Scientists can examine chunks of DNA lifted from blood, hair, skin, or tissue, to find out who someone is, or whether they are related to someone else. This is called DNA typing.

In this photograph the pieces of DNA are shown as dark bands, like a grocery store barcode. Different DNA prints can be compared to find a match.

DNA from the **nucleus** of a cell is fragile, and is often hard to read when it comes from old remains. A more stable source of DNA is found in the mitochondria—the part of a cell that produces its energy. However, mitochondrial DNA can only indicate maternal (mother's-side) relationships.

FILE CLOSED

The Fake Vermeer

Possibly the greatest art forger of all time was Hans van Meegeren (1889–1947). Van Meegeren was not content with copying a great painting and trying to pass it off as the original. So, he actually created original works and sold them as new discoveries of old masters. As well as his own work, van Meegeren specialized in forging the work of fellow Dutchman and celebrated artist, Johannes Vermeer (1632–1675).

Fooling the experts

During the 1930s van Meegeren faked six Vermeer paintings in all, giving them titles such as *The Washing of Christ's Feet*, *Christ and the Adulteress*, and *Lady and Gentleman at a Spinet*. Most famous of all, and generally considered to be van Meegeren's masterpiece, was *Christ at Emmaus*. This painting was bought for a large sum by Boymans Museum in Rotterdam in 1937.

This is the faked painting that van Meegeren showed to Abraham Bredius. *Christ at Emmaus.*

Art historian Abraham Bredius wrote about *Christ at Emmaus* in the *Burlington Magazine* in 1937: "It is a wonderful moment in the life of a lover of art when he finds himself suddenly confronted with a hitherto unknown painting by a great master, untouched, on the original canvas, and without any restoration, just as it left the painter's studio! And what a picture! . . . [W]hat we have here is a—I am inclined to say—*the* masterpiece of Johannes Vermeer of Delft."

A victim of his own success

During World War II van Meegeren sold another "Vermeer," *Christ and the Adulteress*, to **Nazi Reich Marshal** and art collector Hermann Göring. In May 1945 van Meegeren was arrested and charged with treason for having sold a Dutch national treasure—a Vermeer painting—to the enemy. After six weeks in jail, he announced that he had painted the "Vermeer," and had in fact conned Göring with a fake. Not only that, but he had painted five other so-called "Vermeers."

```
How he did it
```
Van Meegeren went to great lengths to make his paintings as authentic-looking as possible. For *Christ at Emmaus* he followed this procedure:

1. He obtained a genuine 17th-century painting with its original stretcher (the wooden frame over which a canvas is stretched).

2. He painted over the original artwork, preparing a fresh surface, which he used for his own painting.

3. Once the painting was complete, he used an aging process he had invented that fooled all the experts. He ground his **pigments** in lilac oil and then mixed them in a particular kind of resin dissolved in a colorless oil called turpentine.

4. He then baked the painting for several hours at a temperature of more than 212°F (100°C).

The effect of Van Meegeren's procedure was to give his work the appearance of a genuine 17th-century painting.

Prove it!

Van Meegeren's announcement was greeted with amazement and disbelief. In the fall of 1945, to prove his claim to the court, van Meegeren was locked in a room with a police guard and six witnesses, to paint another "Vermeer." After two months in the room he produced another excellent Vermeer **forgery,** *Young Christ.*

Forensic tests

Young Christ was still not enough to convince many experts, and the court called for a **forensic analysis** to decide for certain whether van Meegeren was telling the truth. In June 1946, Dr. P. B. Coremans, director of the Central Laboratory of Belgian Museums, was called in. He carried out extensive physical and chemical tests on a number of paintings and materials found in van Meegeren's studio. Coremans found that van Meegeren had used paints containing traces of cobalt blue, an artificial **pigment** not available until the 19th century. **X-rays** also showed original 17th-century paintings under his paintings.

X-ray analysis

X-rays are rays made of the same **electromagnetic** particles as light, but with a much shorter **wavelength.** These shorter wavelengths allow

This is an X-ray photograph of a painting.

X-rays to pass through solid objects, such as the surface of a painting, to show what lies beneath. Radiographers (X-ray specialists) are often called upon to **authenticate** works of art. To investigate the van Meegeren forgeries, Coremans used a kind of X-ray process called **stereoradiography,** which operates at the same wavelength as used to see inside the human body.

Imprisonment

In September 1947, Coremans reported that the paintings were indeed forgeries. The treason charge was dropped. However, the discovery produced anger and dismay in the art world. Göring had not been the only customer to be taken in by the faked Vermeers, and van Meegeren had made a great deal of money out of his deception.

What was more, he had made fools of several well-known art experts. In October 1947 van Meegeren was tried and convicted of forgery, and sentenced to a year's imprisonment. He died of a heart attack two months later.

Analyzing the paint

Paint is made up of various parts, such as pigments, extenders (substances that dilute or add body to a product), and binding media (materials that make pigments stick to a painted surface). A **forensic** scientist can study these parts in order to reach conclusions about the date or origin of a painting because some components would not have been available before a particular time in history, and their presence or absence therefore helps to date a painting.

Today, forensic scientists can use techniques such as **gas chromatography**, a process that separates a substance into the parts that make it up.

Coremans used the tools available to him at the time, such as a polarized light microscope (PLM). A PLM analyzes changes in the quality of light passing through a sample of paint, and by doing so can give clues to its identity.

This forensic chemist is looking at the results of gas chromatography carried out on a paint sample in a 3-D graph.

Counterfeit Currency

FILE OPEN

Fabio Mendes began his **counterfeiting** career in 1970, working out of a friend's house in Bogotá, Colombia. His friend operated a small printing press that he used to run a legitimate (legal and honest) printing business during the day, producing leaflets, posters, and stickers. At night it produced U.S. $100 bills, which Fabio then sold on the streets of Bogotá.

Making money

During the late 1970s and early 1980s, Fabio's counterfeiting business took off, and over the years he sold fake $100 bills worth several million dollars. He was part of a large industry: between 1985 and 2000, more than $100 million of U.S. counterfeit dollars passed into circulation in Colombia.

Paper and ink

For counterfeiting, the materials and equipment are very important. For paper Fabio used $1 bills, because they had the right weight and texture. He washed them clean of ink using bleach. Some counterfeiters saved money by using Venezuelan bolivar notes. But Fabio took pride in his workmanship, preferring to pay more for paper of the right quality.

This **forensic** scientist is checking the **authenticity** of paper currency.

Inks also varied in quality and price. Many counterfeiters were content with the cheapest inks. But these could smear easily. Fabio preferred to spend more on special magnetic and security inks, similar to the ones used to print real $1 bills. These inks could cost more than $750 per kilo.

The printing process

Fabio used a traditional method of printing known as **offset printing**:

1. He created actual-size photographic negatives of the front and back of a $100 bill.

2. With great care, he touched up each negative.

3. When they were ready, the images on the negatives were burned onto a series of light-sensitive aluminum plates. A light was shone through the non-image areas of the negative and burned itself onto the light-sensitive solution that covered the aluminum plate.

4. The plates were attached to the printing press, and the bleached $1 bills were run through the press.

Fabio was prepared to waste a lot of paper at the start of a print run, working to get the ink levels right. "After that," he said, "it's like making bread rolls."

This is an offset printing press like the one used by Fabio to make fake $100 bills.

Traditional values

During the 1990s, many commercial printers began to swap their traditional methods for **digital scanners** and computers. But Fabio continued to use mechanical printing methods. This was partly because of the high cost of computer equipment, but also because the outstanding craftsmanship of his work would be difficult to match using computers.

Beating the counterfeiters

In 1996, the United States Treasury attempted to strike back at counterfeiters by introducing a new range of high-tech elements to their bills, making them harder to copy. They used an **optically variable ink** that appeared either black or green depending on which direction one viewed it from. The new bills also included a larger portrait, a **watermark,** and **microprinting.** There are several methods of microprinting. In one method, a **laser** beam is focused on paper covered with a thin metal film. The laser beam bumps the metal causing it to bond with the paper, and a printed pattern forms.

All these changes made Fabio's job much more difficult. Watermarks, for example, were impossible to copy exactly and microprinting details were very difficult to achieve.

Special **pigments** are used in optically variable ink, so that the color changes if you observe it at an angle of 30 to 40 degrees.

Public trust

By 2000, Fabio was no longer producing fake bills, but worked in the multi-million-dollar distribution industry that moved the **counterfeit** money from the producers in Colombia, to New York, Miami, Buenos Aires, Tokyo, London, and Madrid. He admitted to *The New York Times'* reporter that life was harder these days for counterfeiters. Still, the one factor counterfeiters always had on their side was the public's trust in the bills they carried in their wallets. Very few people inspect their money close enough to observe whether it was real or fake. Fabio had not been caught at the time of the interview in 2000.

New technology

Science and technology have been used in various ways to make currency harder to counterfeit:

- Optically variable ink: it looks green when viewed straight on, but looks black at an angle. Color-shifting ink was used in the numeral in the bottom-right corner of some notes in the 1996 U.S. redesign.

- Microprinting: to the naked eye it appears as a thin line on many of the 1996 bills, but under a magnifying glass the lettering can easily be seen. Yet most **offset printers** or copying machines are unable to copy the detail of such fine print.

- Holograms: a new anti-counterfeiting idea that is being introduced around the world is the addition of a 3-D **hologram** using advanced reflective foils.

Holograms are an expensive, but highly effective security feature. The image changes according to the angle of viewing, and multiple colors are often used.

The Howard Hughes Hoax

FILE OPEN

One day in 1971 a writer named Clifford Irving approached the McGraw-Hill Book Company with a literary sensation. He announced that he had been granted permission to write the biography, or life story, of Howard Hughes, the world-famous multimillionaire, movie-maker, and eccentric. The publishers were amazed. Hughes had not been seen in public for years, and there had been several rumors of his death. Irving showed them a letter that he said was written by Hughes, giving him access to talk to the great man. The editors at McGraw-Hill were convinced by Irving's story and the letter, and paid him $765,000 for the right to publish the book.

The perfect subject

In fact, Irving had never met Hughes. He had made up the whole story, and forged the letter himself. Irving had calculated that Hughes, being both famous and invisible, was the perfect subject for this scheme. On the one hand, the public was hungry for information about Hughes, and on the other hand, no one could deny the biography was genuine.

During his research for the book, Irving came across a copy of Hughes' handwriting, and used that as a basis for his forged letter. On two separate occasions McGraw-Hill hired graphologists (handwriting experts) to check the **authenticity** of the handwriting, and both experts concluded that the letter was indeed written by Hughes.

Irving told McGraw-Hill that Hughes also required payment for the book, and the publishers sent regular checks to Irving,

Clifford Irving claimed that he had met Howard Hughes more than a hundred times to tape-record his life story.

payable to H. R. Hughes. Irving's wife opened a Swiss bank account under that name and deposited the checks.

Pure fiction

Irving delivered the 900-page manuscript, based—he claimed—on written records of lengthy telephone conversations between himself and Hughes. When in fact he had drawn on magazine articles, and interviews Hughes had given during his more public years, mixed in with completely fictitious details. *LIFE* magazine believed the manuscript to be authentic, and bought the rights to publish passages from the book before it was released.

Handwriting analysis

Experienced handwriting analysts can spot the differences between handwriting samples which look to most of us as if they are written by the same person. A person's handwriting has certain characteristics that remain present throughout adult life. Someone attempting to copy that style may manage a superficial likeness, but on closer inspection differences will show up. Indications of disguised writing include:

- shaky formation of letters
- awkward pen movements
- stops and starts in odd places
- careful repair of wrongly formed letters.

It is easier to copy the overall shape of someone's handwriting than it is the details like pen pressure and connecting strokes. The small details depend on the structure of the actual hand.

This handwriting analyst uses a computer linked to a microscope to enhance the clarity of a sample to make it easier to study.

Telephone conference

When McGraw-Hill and *LIFE* announced their **"scoop,"** the real Howard Hughes was enraged. He was even prepared to break his fifteen-year silence so that he could personally deny any connection with the book. A telephone press conference was arranged through the broadcasting organization NBC. Hughes gave the conference from his luxury hideaway on Paradise Island in the Bahamas, to a group of reporters in a Los Angeles hotel.

The reporters' first task was to establish the **authenticity** of the voice on the other end of the telephone. The first questions were answered easily enough. Then one reporter reminded him of his round-the-world trip in 1938 when a woman placed a good-luck charm on his airplane. "What was it," the reporter asked, "and where was it placed?"

There was a long silence at the other end of the phone. "I have to be completely honest with you," came the voice eventually. "I don't remember that one." But before the reporter could finish his next question, the voice interrupted: he recalled it now—the woman had stuck a wad of chewing gum to the tail of his plane. All the other reporters' questions were answered to their satisfaction, convincing them that they were talking to the real Howard Hughes.

Hughes then launched into an attack on Irving's book. ". . . I don't know [Irving]. I never saw him," he said. "I have never even heard of him until a matter of days ago when this thing first came to my attention."

A perfect match

When the telephone conference was made public, Irving immediately declared the caller an impostor, describing the voice

This newspaper headline was published after Irving confessed. In June 1972, he was found guilty of **forgery** and was sentenced to 30 months in jail.

as "much too vigorous and deep . . ." However, NBC had expected Irving's claim, and had hired **voiceprint** expert Lawrence Kersta to analyze the tape. Kersta found that the voice on the phone perfectly matched a recording of Hughes' voice in a speech he had made 30 years earlier to a Senate subcommittee. A second expert agreed with Kersta's conclusion.

Game over

From this point on, Irving's **hoax** began to fall apart very quickly. The Swiss banking authorities, suspicious of the woman in dark glasses who had opened the H. R. Hughes account, launched their own **investigation.** They handed documents containing handwriting, supposedly by Hughes, to the Crime Laboratory of the Postal Inspection Service in New York. After close examination, differences were found between Hughes' handwriting and Irving's imitation of it.

Voiceprint analysis

The match that Kersta had found between the voice on the tape and Hughes' speech 30 years earlier proved his theory that although voices change over time, their special quality remains constant. His first task when comparing the voices was to convert the tapes into **spectrograms,** or voice pictures, measuring such aspects as pitch, tone, and volume. He then compared the voice pictures from each tape line by line.

Voiceprint spectrograms can be viewed on computer screen, or as printouts. They show horizontal lines of constantly varying width that measure a voice's pitch, tone, and volume.

This is a printout of a spectrogram, showing the basic patterns of pitch, tone. and intensity that make each voice unique.

The Hitler Diaries

> In February 1981, Gerd Heidemann, a journalist at the German magazine, *Stern*, handed the directors of the magazine's parent company, Gruner and Jahr, the publishing **scoop** of the century: the diaries of Adolf Hitler. Heidemann showed them three volumes in black binding, filled with an almost unreadable German handwriting. He told them there were 27 volumes in all, covering the years 1932 to 1945.

The source

Heidemann did not reveal his source, except to say that the diaries came from a wealthy collector of Nazi memorabilia (memorable souvenirs) and brother of an East German general. Heidemann knew this man only as Dr. Fischer, but his real name was Konrad Kujau, born in England in 1938. A petty criminal and talented forger, Kujau had in fact written the diaries himself.

Consulting the experts

Despite the vagueness of Heidemann's story, Gruner and Jahr were prepared to trust him. They agreed to buy the diaries for around three million dollars. Only then did Gruner and Jahr submit the diaries for **authentication.** The two handwriting experts they consulted both agreed that the diaries were genuine. This was not surprising because the "genuine" samples of Hitler's handwriting the experts were given to compare the diaries against came from the same source as the diaries: Konrad Kujau!

The first pages of Hitler's diary were published in *Stern* on April 25, 1983, the day Gruner and Jahr announced their scoop.

Gruner and Jahr began paying Heidemann huge sums of cash for him to pass on to his source. Heidemann kept a lot of the money for himself, and began buying expensive cars and houses. However, none of his fellow journalists appeared to notice the rapid rise in his standard of living.

Media frenzy

Gruner and Jahr announced their scoop in April 1983, and the diaries instantly captured the world's attention. Historians considered how the diaries might completely change our understanding of the Nazi leader. The magazine *Newsweek* competed with Rupert Murdoch's media empire for the right to publish the diaries internationally.

Murdoch asked the respected British historian and world-renowned authority on Hitler, Hugh Trevor-Roper (later Lord Dacre), to examine the diaries. Under pressure from the German publishers, he announced that, in his view, the diaries were genuine. Trevor-Roper later admitted he had been overwhelmed by the huge quantity of material placed before him. He had also been influenced by the fact that the handwriting had already been authenticated. Trevor-Roper thought the diaries were real, but he had been swayed toward that conclusion.

Gerd Heidemann (right) is pictured with Wolf Hess, son of Nazi leader Rudolf Hess, holding one of Hitler's diaries.

The forger

Konrad Kujau embarked on his criminal career in the 1960s, **forging** lunch tickets (tickets given by employers to staff to exchange for lunch).

From there he went on to forging paintings and Nazi memorabilia, and ultimately the Hitler diaries. Kujau had convinced Heidemann that the diaries had been rescued from the wreckage of a plane carrying Hitler's personal property, which had crashed in Dresden in 1945. He told him the diaries had been secretly stored for more than three decades by his brother, an East German general, before being smuggled into West Germany in the late 1970s.

Forensic investigation

By the time Trevor-Roper reached his verdict, the West German authorities knew the diaries were fakes. Government **forensic** scientists had conducted their own **investigation** into the diaries, this time concentrating on the paper and ink. Under **ultraviolet** light, the paper in six of the diaries was shown to contain a whitening agent called blankophor, which had not come into use until after 1954. The book bindings also contained whitener, and threads attached to the seals were made from viscose and polyester, both post-war materials. But the biggest giveaway was the ink. By measuring the evaporation of chloride **solvent** from the ink, the document examiners could establish that the 1943 diary had been written less than twelve months ago!

This person is analyzing the age of ink by paper chromatography. The components in the ink show up as different colored circles.

Trevor-Roper wrote an article for the *Sunday Times* declaring his belief in the diaries. At the last moment, however, the historian began to have doubts. He called the publisher, requesting that the paper remove his article, but he was too late—it was already being printed.

Exposure

On May 6, 1983, German government scientists announced that the diaries were crude **forgeries.** For Gruner and Jahr this news was a financial disaster, costing them somewhere in the region of twenty million marks (thirteen million dollars). For Gerd Heidemann, who had been convinced all along that the diaries were genuine, it was a personal humiliation. It also meant his exposure as a criminal, since about 1.7 million marks (one million dollars) of the fee for the diaries had found its way into his account. In 1985, he was convicted of misappropriating (using incorrectly) his employer's money, and received a prison sentence of four years and eight months. Konrad Kujau was sentenced to four years and six months.

Gathering forensic evidence

Forensic document examiners are often asked to identify and date the paper and ink on a document.

Analyzing paper: a sheet of paper has many physical and chemical properties that can help to identify and date it. Most of the world's paper comes from **wood pulp** obtained by using chemicals to break wood down into its individual fibers. The fiber makeup of paper can be revealed by partially dissolving it in dilute acid and then examining the fibers under a microscope. The fibers have individual characteristics that can often tell you which wood they came from.

Ink dating: as ink ages on paper, a certain ingredient in the ink known as the solvent gradually evaporates. The rate of this evaporation can be expressed as a curve if drawn on a graph: it is most rapid when the ink is fresh, then it slows down, and finally it levels off. Different ink types have different evaporation rate curves. One way of dating ink is to use **gas chromatography** to measure the quantity of the solvent, and then check this against the evaporation curve of that particular ink.

Documents can be analyzed by taking ink samples from the paper.

Framing the Neighbor

Graham Backhouse was a failure as a farmer. Within a few years of taking over at Widden Hall Farm in Somerset, England, he had built up massive debts thanks to successive crop failures and his bad spending habits. Not only that, but Backhouse—a married man—had angered his neighbors in the village of Horton, by openly flirting with several local women.

In March 1984, a sheep's head was found fixed on Backhouse's fence with a note attached: "You next." Backhouse went to the local police station, claiming this was merely the latest incident in a long hate campaign against him, including abusive letters and threatening phone calls.

The car bomb

On April 9, Backhouse asked his wife Margaret to drive into town to pick up some medicine for his livestock. Her own car would not start, so she took her husband's car instead. When she started the car, a bomb, hidden beneath the driver's seat, exploded, causing serious injury to her thigh and thousands of deep, jagged cuts all over her body. Screaming with pain, she managed to crawl from the wrecked car. Backhouse failed to respond to her cries. He was some way off in the cowshed with the radio at full volume. Luckily she was spotted by some passengers on a passing bus, and was rushed to the hospital.

Graham Backhouse, a 44-year-old former hairdresser, was an unpopular figure in Horton.

Explosives experts examined the wreckage and found evidence of a simple but deadly device. The bomb had been made from a length of steel pipe packed with nitroglycerine (explosive liquid) and shotgun pellets, and was wired to go off when the engine was switched on.

Threatening letter

Soon after, Backhouse reported receiving another threatening letter. This note, along with the previous one, was sent to Mike Hall, a document examiner at the Birmingham **Forensic** Laboratory. Hall observed that each letter in the second note had been gone over backward and forward several times, making it impossible to identify the handwriting. When he turned his attention to the "You next" note, Hall noticed the faint impression of a doodle on the back, probably made on the previous sheet in the notepad. He filed it away for future reference.

Analyzing impressions

The impressions made by a pen pressing on paper can go through several sheets. To see these impressions more clearly:

1. cover the paper with a thin sheet of plastic, similar to plastic wrap

2. give the sheet an **electrostatic** charge in order to creates an invisible electrostatic image on the sheet

3. pour black powder (like toner from a copy machine) over the sheet; the static charge makes it stick to the image area

4. discard the excess powder, leaving a clear image of the marks made by the pen.

Black powder is about to be poured over this plastic-covered sheet of paper in order to reveal any impressions on the paper.

Trouble with the neighbor

Backhouse told the police that he suspected his neighbor, Colin Bedale-Taylor, of planting the bomb. The two men had been engaged in a lengthy dispute over a right of way, and 63-year-old Bedale-Taylor had been depressed since the death of his son in a car accident two years before.

Backhouse was given round-the-clock police protection at his farm. Nine days later, Backhouse ordered their removal, claiming he was quite able to defend himself—he had a shotgun. The police withdrew, warning him not to take the law into his own hands. An alarm button was installed at Widden Hall Farm, with a direct connection to the local police station. On the evening of April 30 the alarm was sounded.

Knife attack

The police raced over, and found Backhouse just inside his front doorway covered in blood. His face had been slashed several times down one side, and a deep cut ran from his left shoulder diagonally across his body. At his feet lay the dead body of Colin Bedale-Taylor, killed by two shotgun blasts. A bloodstained Stanley knife lay in the dead man's hand.

Backhouse described what had happened. Bedale-Taylor had come on a neighborly visit to enquire about Margaret's health. They were in the kitchen when Bedale-Taylor had suddenly gone mad, crying out that God had sent him. He admitted planting the bomb, but said it was in revenge for his son's death, which he blamed on Backhouse. He then attacked Backhouse with the Stanley knife, and Backhouse fought him off before running to the hall to get his shotgun. Bedale-Taylor ran toward him and Backhouse shot him, then shot him again.

The police were initially inclined to believe Backhouse's story. Further evidence was found to support Backhouse's description of events: the Stanley knife was engraved with the initials "BT," and during a police search of Bedale-Taylor's house the steel pipe was found from which the car bomb had been made.

Crime scene analysis

However, certain odd features at the crime scene puzzled **forensic** scientists. For example, there was no blood trail between the kitchen and the hall, where Backhouse said he ran to get his gun. Also, Backhouse had no wounds on his hands. Hand wounds are normally found on someone defending themselves from a knife attack.

Blood drops

The patterns made by drops and splashes of blood on walls, floors, and clothing, can help forensic scientists create a picture of events at a crime scene.

In the case of Graham Backhouse, it was noticed that the shape of the blood drops on the kitchen floor did not match Backhouse's story.

During a fight or struggle, blood drops land with characteristic tails, due to movement. Yet these blood drops were simple round circles, as if they had dripped from someone standing still.

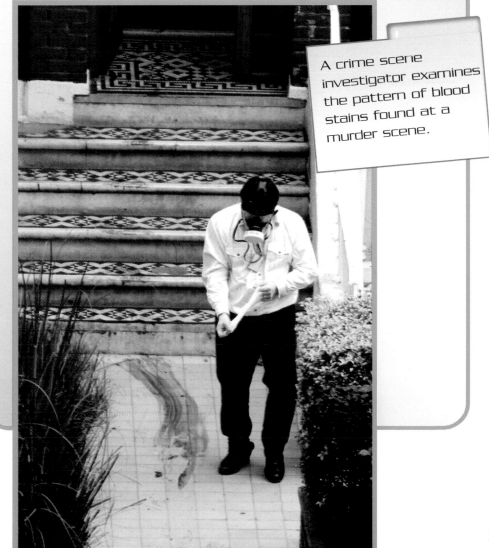

A crime scene investigator examines the pattern of blood stains found at a murder scene.

Stanley knife mystery

There was another mysterious difference: Bedale-Taylor, a carpenter, had engraved his initials with great care on all his tools, but the initials on the Stanley knife had been crudely and hurriedly carved.

Dr. William Kennard was the pathologist (scientist who determines the cause of death) on the case. He was perplexed by the fact that the Stanley knife was found clasped in the fingers of the corpse, rather than lying on the floor. This could only have happened, he said, if rigor mortis (the stiffening of the body that occurs several hours after death) had taken place immediately—a physical impossibility. It was beginning to look as if Backhouse had killed Bedale-Taylor, and then placed the knife in his hand.

The wool fiber

Gradually, evidence accumulated to show that Backhouse had also faked the hate campaign against himself. An examination of the envelope containing the first threatening letter revealed a tiny wool fiber stuck to the flap. The fiber was carefully analyzed and was found to have come from Backhouse's own wool sweater, suggesting that he had sent the letter to himself. The impression of a doodle that Mike Hall had found on the back of the "You Next" note matched a doodle on a notebook found at Widden Hall Farm.

It soon emerged that Backhouse was even responsible for the car bomb that had nearly killed his wife. In early March, he had increased Margaret's life insurance from £50,000 to £100,000 ($100,000 to $200,000). The money he would have received had she died would have helped him pay off his debts.

Backhouse had launched the fake hate campaign, and a few weeks later, had

Margaret Backhouse, wife of Graham Backhouse, was badly injured by a car bomb planted by her husband.

planted the bomb. To escape suspicion, he decided to frame Bedale-Taylor. He persuaded him to come to his house, where he killed him and took measures to make it look as if Bedale-Taylor had attacked him first. On the outside, Backhouse appeared to be innocent; and it was only through patient **forensic** detection that the truth of his crimes emerged.

Desperate ploy

Backhouse continued to scheme even while he was in prison awaiting trial. He persuaded a fellow inmate to send an unsigned letter to a local newspaper stating that Bedale-Taylor had been responsible for the car bomb. The plot failed when the handwriting was analyzed and found to be that of the prisoner. On February 18, 1985, Backhouse was convicted of murder and sentenced to two terms of life imprisonment.

Analysis of fibers

Every type of fiber, wool, cotton, or manmade, has its own unique structure, and the type of material can be identified by examining a piece of fiber under a high-powered microscope.

For more detailed analysis—say, to match a wool fiber to a particular sweater—other methods are required, such as **infrared spectrometry.** With this technique, the degree of absorption of infrared light passing through a fiber is measured and displayed as an image. This is called a "signature," and it can be compared to a library of other "signatures," enabling the fiber to be identified.

Fibers can be examined under a microscope to reveal details of their shape, weave pattern, and strand size.

Stolen Identity

In July 1998 some fishermen from Devonshire, England, found the body of a man trapped in their fishing nets. They reported their gruesome discovery to the local police. The body was in bad condition, having been submerged for some time in 67 feet (20 meters) of water, and the police found nothing on the man to indicate his identity. The only clue they had was the Rolex watch on his wrist.

Rolex to the rescue

This turned out to be a lucky break, because Rolex keeps records of all its customers. Inscribed inside the watch were details of when it was serviced. Through this, Rolex was able to give the police the man's name—Ronald Platt—and his address at the time the watch was serviced.

Every Rolex can be traced back to its owner.

Police made inquiries and discovered that, according to official records, Platt was still alive and well. His credit cards and bank accounts were still being used. The **forensic** team came to the conclusion that someone had killed Platt and stolen his identity. But who?

The cell phone number

The police visited the address supplied by Rolex, and through patient detective work, eventually arrived at Platt's last known residence. The owner of the property confirmed that Platt had lived there. He was asked for contact details of any of Platt's friends or family. He gave police the cell phone number of David Davies, a man who had provided him with a reference for Platt. When police called this number, they had no idea they were speaking to Platt's murderer.

A man of many names

David Davies was one of the names used by Albert Walker, a crooked businessman, who had swindled a lot of people out of their money, and was wanted by Interpol (an international organization of police forces). He befriended Ronald Platt, an Englishman who had spent his childhood in Canada and wished to go back there. Walker paid for Platt's return to Canada, but before he left he stole Platt's birth certificate and driver's license.

This allowed Walker to live as Platt, and he would have continued to do so if the real Platt had not decided to come back to England and live nearby. Realizing he was in danger of exposure, Walker decided to murder Platt. He persuaded Platt to come on board his yacht where Walker killed him. His one mistake was to leave the Rolex on Platt's wrist. Walker was convicted of murder and sentenced to life imprisonment.

Cause of death

With the discovery of a dead body, one of the most important questions that forensic scientists must ask themselves is, "How did he or she die?"

The Forensic Science Service, based at Chepstow in South Wales, England, examined the body of Ronald Platt and they found:

The color of a bruise can tell a medical examiner how old it is. Over the course of two weeks, bruises change from red, to blue or purple, to green, to yellow, and finally to brown.

1. bruises on his body that covered an area exactly the same length as the shaft of the anchor.

2. traces of zinc from the anchor on Platt's belt, which had been badly stretched.

3. leather fibers from the belt on the anchor.

From this evidence, the experts deduced that the anchor had been stuffed into the belt of Platt's pants and used to weigh him down in the water. This new theory led them to conclude that Platt had been murdered.

Solve It!

So, you have read the book. You have seen the professionals in action. Now solve this mystery. Imagine that you are a **forensic** scientist. You must decide which of the techniques described in the book you would use to solve the following case . . .

A new drug

A dispute has arisen between two distinguished scientists. Both scientists claim to be the inventors of a **formula** for a new drug to treat high blood pressure, which could be worth millions of dollars. In the spring of 2000, Professor Fish publishes an article describing his discovery in a scientific journal.

Shortly after, Fish is sued by his former teacher, Professor Hook. Hook claims that *he* came up with the very same formula fifteen years before, and that Professor Fish stole it from him. To prove it, Hook has unearthed several sheets of handwritten notes that he claims were written in 1985, describing in great detail his experiments with the drug.

The witness

To strengthen his case, Hook has also found a witness—Ms. Angler—who is willing to state in court that she assisted Hook with his experiments in 1985. Indeed, the records from the time show that Ms. Angler was a graduate student employed as a part-time laboratory assistant at the university between 1984 and 1986. The university also possesses in its **archives** a videotape of a meeting of the Chemistry Society in October 1985, at which Ms. Angler delivered a paper. The videotape includes close-ups of Ms. Angler both face-on and in profile. Ms. Angler left the university in 1986, and went to live overseas. All records of her cease after that point.

Is Hook a liar?

Professor Fish is outraged at Hook's assertions. He regards Hook as a jealous old rival, who is trying to steal the glory from his more talented student He does not believe that Hook was involved in research of this nature back then. The notes that Hook has conveniently "rediscovered" must have been written after Fish's article was published. Even if it could be proved that the notes were written in 1985, nothing would convince him that Hook had written them himself, since. As for Ms. Angler, Fish has a distinct recollection of her having a longer nose, and he is certain that the person Hook is now putting forward as a witness is a different woman entirely.

What you must do

You are a private forensic investigator, hired by Professor Fish's legal team. Your job is to:

1. determine when the notes were written

2. decide whether Professor Hook wrote the notes

3. establish whether Hook's witness is indeed the same Ms. Angler who assisted him in 1985.

What techniques will you use in this case?

ANSWERS

1. Identify the ink used by using a technique such as **thin-layer chromatography**. Then, find out the age of the ink on the paper by measuring the quantity of **solvent** it contains using **gas chromatography**, and checking this against the evaporation curve for that particular ink.

2. Obtain a sample of Professor Hook's handwriting and compare it with the handwriting on the notes.

3. Examine stills from the videotape showing close-ups of Ms. Angler in profile, and compare the shape of her ear with that of the ear of the woman claiming to be her now. Compare **spectrograms** of the two women's voices.

Glossary

archive catalog and items in a collection

authentication establishing that something is real or true

authenticity realness or truth of something

beta radiography use of beta rays to test the density of materials like paper. Beta rays are electrons given off during the decay of certain radioactive isotopes. Beta rays are less penetrating than X-rays, and are easily turned aside by paper fibers.

cartilage tough, elastic tissue found in the nose, ear, throat, and other parts of the body

cell smallest independent unit in an organism

counterfeit copy of something, especially money, made to deceive people

digital imaging technology use of devices, like scanners, to convert images into digital form

digital scanner device used to convert an image into a digital form (i.e. represented in numerical digits) in order to store, retrieve, or transmit it

DNA molecule in the form of a twisted double strand (a double helix) found in every cell of every living thing. It is a major component of chromosomes (rod-shaped structures in a cell nucleus) and carries genetic information (this determines an organism's characteristics).

DNA typing forensic method of identifying a person by analyzing their DNA

electromagnetic created by electromagnetism, which is magnetism produced by an electric current

electrostatic produced by static electricity, which is a stationary electric charge that builds up on an insulated object

forensic relating to the application of science in the course of a criminal investigation

forensic analysis detailed scientific examination for the purpose of providing evidence for use in a court of law

forgery illegal copies of paintings, money, etc.

formula group of chemical symbols that show what a substance consists of

fraud crime of obtaining money or some other benefit by deliberate deception

gas chromatography analyzing the components of a gas by injecting it into the stream of another inert (non-reactive) gas and into a long, thin tube that slows down each component. As the components emerge one by one at the end of the tube, they pass through a detector that analyzes them.

hoax attempt to make people believe that something fake is real

hologram three-dimensional image of an object

infrared   part of the electromagnetic spectrum (the complete range of radiation), invisible to the human eye, consisting of radiation with wavelengths between those of light and radio waves

infrared luminescence   infrared light can be used to view inks that have been erased or written over. For example, some inks that appear brightly colored in normal light may be transparent in infrared light. In contrast, some inks, invisible in ordinary light, appear luminescent, or shiny, under infrared light. This effect, known as infrared luminescence, may be observed through a device that converts the luminescence into a visible image.

infrared spectrometry   method used to measure how much infrared light is absorbed when passing through a transparent substance. This measurement, called a "signature," can be compared to the "signatures" of other known substances as a way of identifying the unknown substance.

investigation   formal inquiry to find out as much information as possible about something

laser   device that uses the ability of certain substances to absorb electromagnetic energy, which it then re-radiates as a highly focused beam of single-wavelength radiation

microprinting   technique of printing text so small that it has to be magnified to be viewed

mitochondrial DNA   form of DNA found in the mitochondria, the structures that produce a cell's energy. Mitochondrial DNA is harder to test than ordinary DNA and can only indicate relationships through the maternal line. However, because it is tougher than DNA from a cell nucleus, it can be found in very old remains and provides important information about archaeological finds.

Nazi Reich Marshal   leading figure in the Nazi regime that ruled Germany from 1933 to 1945

nucleus   spherical body at the center of a cell that contains the genetic information necessary to control cell growth and reproduction

offset printing   method of printing in which inked impressions are transferred onto paper from another surface

optically variable ink   ink that appears to change color, depending on the angle from which it is viewed

pigment   substance that is added to give something, such as paint or ink, its color

questioned document   any handwritten, typed, or printed item that a forensic document examiner studies to assess its authenticity

scoop important piece of news that usually only one newspaper publishes

solvent substance—usually a liquid—in which other substances can be dissolved

spectrogram graphical representation of a spectrum or range, such as the range of a voice

stereoradiography process in which two X-ray photographs are taken of the same area at the same time but from different angles in order to reconstruct the shape of something, such as a bone

thin-layer chromatography form of chromatography in which the components of a liquid are separated from each other. A sample of a liquid is extracted in a solvent, which is placed on a glass plate coated with a thin layer of a substance called alumina (colorless aluminum oxide). The components travel at different speeds along the glass plate because of differences in their chemical composition.

ultraviolet part of the electromagnetic spectrum (the complete range of radiation), consisting of radiation with wavelengths beyond the violet end of the visible light spectrum

voiceprint graph that shows in picture form the patterns of a voice

watermark design or mark incorporated within paper during its manufacture that can be seen when it is held up to the light

wavelength distance between two points on waves (such as radio waves or light waves) that are next to each other

wood pulp wood that has been mechanically and chemically broken down for use in making paper and paper products

X-ray high-energy electromagnetic radiation with a wavelength that is capable of penetrating solid objects

Get into Forensics

Forensics is a complex and fascinating business. Investigators may be called upon to make identifications from DNA fragments, take fingerprints from a crime scene, check photographs for fakes, examine paper fibers under an electron microscope, find the age of ancient bones using radiocarbon dating, match tire tracks left by a getaway car, or compare known dental records to the corpse of an unknown person.

One person alone cannot master such a wide range of skills, and those involved in forensic investigations often perform highly specialized tasks. Ballistics experts, for example, will match projectiles with weapons and detect traces of explosives on fabric or skin. Toxicologists may be called on by a pathologist carrying out an autopsy to examine a particular organ for indications of a hard-to-detect poison.

In their way of working, all forensic investigators are scientific or medical professionals. In fact, the range of skills required is so broad it covers almost every aspect of science and medicine: physics, chemistry, biology, medicine and dentistry, anthropology, archaeology, and psychology. So any reader wanting to pursue a career in forensics will need to begin with an interest in science.

Useful Websites

A website that gives details of the criminal mind and the methods they use:
    http://www.crimelibrary.com/index.html

A site that gives detailed articles about various crime scene investigator techniques and tools:
    http://www.crime-scene-investigator.net/

The FBI's website for young adults:
    http://www.fbi.gov/kids/6th12th/6th12th.htm

A website updated daily about hoaxes, pranks, and fakes of all kinds:
    http://www.museumofhoaxes.com/

Further Reading

Innes, Brian. *Forensic Science.* Broomall, Penn.: Mason Crest Publishers, 2002.

Jackson, Donna M. *The Bone Detectives: How Forensic Anthropologists Solve Crimes and Uncover Mysteries of the Dead.* Boston: Little Brown & Company, 1996.

Pentland, Peter and Pennie Stoyles. *Forensic Science.* Broomall, Penn.: Chelsea House Publishers, 2003.

Woodford, Chris. *Criminal Investigation.* Chicago: Raintree, 2001.

Index